Poet Reflects Your World

Laurie Wilkinson

The Psychy Poet

This edition published in Great Britain in 2019 by MyVoice Publishing

www.MyVoicePublishing.com

ISBN

Cover Photo:

Introduction

I suppose I could say that if my previous books were "Six of the Best", then this latest one before you will make "The Magnificent Seven", though perhaps that is a bit twee. But hey, I have said it now so I will state that I'm very confident you will indeed find this my latest and seventh book, "magnificent".

Well having boldly stated my faith in this book I guess I should give some reasons for that so here we go then, and they can also give some indication of my involvements since my last book was published in October 2018. Happily all of my book sales are continuing to go well and certainly beyond my initial wildest dreams!

So, in the last 18 months I have had three of my poems read out live, and many more complimented, on national radio that broadcasts internationally too. I have seen my bookings for my "poetry reading" Gigs increase, with many on recommendation, also my "Book Five" was runner up in a "book of the Year" competition run by The Sussex Newspaper.

I am now regularly asked to read my poems at prestigious events, and literally in the last six weeks (July/ August 2019) I have won two poetry competitions, and am in running for more. I will refer to the two competition winning poems further on as they are both in this book, but to round this up, all the above were among my many reasons for increased confidence and belief in my poetry, and therefore obviously this book!

Of course all my efforts and raised money still donate to the excellent charity Help for Heroes I continue to support with all of my increasing activities!

So onto the poems included in this book then, and again they follow my popular tried and tested format of romance, humour, reflection and tragedy that affect all our lives. The two competition winning poems are "Humpty Dumpty Revisited", my amusing (fed back) take on the nursery rhyme, and a "powerful and emotional" offering entitled "Letter from Afghanistan".

My romance section offers "Sensations of Love", very well received at my gigs, "Desert" and "Praising Naughty Girls", err yes!

The improbable but true "Diddler on the Roof" and "Leggings Don't Lie" are in the humour section with "Damsons and Distress", which may also amuse, and Wedding Dress" reflective section poems. "Absent" and "Bumpy Road" are featured as tragedy offerings, but with so much more in this book....

Increasingly popular poems about my created and still mischievous teddy bears "Ted and Beth", (and their many friends now) are of course included, with "Bears in Love", and "Bears New Friend Tigger" among others here for your amusement.

Anyway I will leave you to explore my new book, and the spectrum of subjects that will surely touch and resonate with you in some way, and indeed all of us as we ride our roller coaster of life.

As ever, please enjoy this my seventh and latest book as "The Journey Continues".....

Laurie Wilkinson Bsc (hons) RMN

Acknowledgements

As this is now my seventh book it is getting much harder to recognise and credit people who deserve it without repeating myself too much. Thus once again I will try for a quick resume, whilst hopefully not missing anybody out!

I do though a need to recognise great and increased support and encouragement from family and friends, and especially my usual "supportive suspects" and also the various groups and organisations that I belong to.

So thanks again to the 42nd Highland Regiment (1815), Anderida Writers Eastbourne, The S East and Eastbourne area "Mumpreneurs", The Sussex Newspaper Online & sister paper Bonjour Limousin Online I write my monthly articles on, (four years now). Local E Sussex businesses, shops, pubs, (many who sell my books), charities and all the wonderful people I meet and liaise with too numerous to mention individually by name.

I must however acknowledge a a few special folks for their amazing support etc, so much gratitude to Elizabeth Wright (The Writer), who "guided and encouraged" me literally from my very start, Mick Seaman, Jane F, Tamara & Andrew, Mick W Senior, The Priory Court Hotel Pevensey, Garden Bar Eastbourne Waterfront for their continued donations and support from my outset too!

The excellent Lynn Parsons of Magic Radio must be thanked for all her fun, endorsements and mentions of me, Nessy & Tracy of regular Gig venues, Seb of Langney Tesco and team, and Richard Milton of E C F car care Eastbourne.

Oh, also La Guingette (means "good time") bar St Eulalie France, Lesley A T, a colleague from the past, Geoff H a long ago school friend, Julie A V and yes Suanne Phillips my "stalwart fan"from S. Africa.

Many, many more must remain unmentioned but not forgotten as you will be thanked elsewhere and perhaps personally......

My Voice Publishing need a mention, as they "suffer and indulge" me as probably "too over enthusiastic", but a determined and growing poetic author for them!

As always my final recognition of gratitude is to you people taking the time to read this book, and with an even bigger thanks to the kind folks who have bought my previous books, and buy this one too, which as ever ensures my donation to the excellent charity Help for Heroes from all my sales.

Thanks again, and bless you all!

Reflections

You may not get true reflections
Unless they are sent back to you,
By astute and impartial eyes
That watch the things you do.

Or maybe it's about your reactions
To experiences of the world you had,
Which always provoke responses
Should they be good or bad.

So indulge comments from neutrals
On your behaviours in the world,
Because you will get genuine views
When their reflections are unfurled.

Contents

Introduction   I
Acknowledgements   III

ROMANCE

Come Our Tomorrow	3
Sensations of Love	4
Desert	6
Flutter	8
Sleepwalking	10
Shiver	12
Close	14
Bears in Love	16
Daisy	18
Praising Naughty Girls	20
One Voice	22
Cut Loose	24
Mary Go Round	26
Gratitude	28
Royal George	30
Loves Illusion Confusion	32
Ted n Beth at Prayer	34
Hypnotic Dance	36
Frozen	38
Desired Effect	40

HUMOUR

No Hiding Place	43
Humpty Dumpty Revisited	44
Up or Down?	46
Diddler on the Roof	48
Bell End	50
Ladies Wait and Queue	52
Bears New Friend Tigger	54
Leggings Don't Tell Lies	56
Fly Past	58
Five Limericks	60
Double Vision	62
Ellie Elephant	64
I Wish I Could Whistle	66
Circus	68
Naked Ambition	70
Big Bruno	72
Neill at the Bar	74
Sofa so Good	76
Handfight at the OK Sauce Table	78
The Lonely Life of a Lemon	80

REFLECTION

Damsons and Distress	85
Inquisition	88
The Man Who Has Seen Everything	90
It's Agony	92
A Grain of Sand	94

Death of a Laptop	96
I Can't Hear You	98
The Bloke Down The Pub	100
Cowboys and Motorists	102
I Hope it Doesn't Rain	104
Pass Me the Remote	106
Conspiracy	109
A Foot in the Grave?	112
I Don't Belong Here	114
Relay Race	116
Wedding Dress	118
Where?	120
Filter	122
Old Remedies	124
Northern Territories Nostalgia	126

TRAGEDY

Letter From Afghanistan	132
Absent	134
Bumpy Road	136
Expiry Date	138
What a Piece of	140
Clown at a Wake	142
With No Warning	144
Blemishes or Insanity?	146
Quiet Joker	148
Bird Songs	150
You Made Your Bed	152
Surfers Against Sewage	154
The Pool and the Leaves	156

Slipping Away   158
Mobilecide   160
Beyond the Facade   162
Don't Turn the Lights Out   164
Fortitude   166
Brexit Wounds   168
A Throw of the Dice   170

APPENDIX   173

More?   178

Laurie Wilkinson

ROMANCE

Come Our Tomorrow

I will have all of your love tomorrow
And share our kisses so very sweet,
For we will always have it all
Each and every time we meet.

I will feel your touch tomorrow
As your hands explore my frame.
Saying you've had private moments
But without me, it's not the same.

I will bring you to life tomorrow
As I gently stroke and softly caress
Your body, just as you like it,
When your secret parts I address.

I will fuel your desire tomorrow
To make you want all you feel,
For until it's just the two of us
Those desired heights aren't real.

I will hold you close tomorrow
As we melt our bodies into one,
To feel that glorious togetherness
When we are finally all done.

But I'm coming for you now my love
Coming for you fast as I can drive,
For I have set desire all aflame
And tomorrow may not arrive!

--ooOoo--

Sensations of Love

From lovestruck teen to an older heart
Love can arrive and catapult you,
To unscaled heights and sensations
With many vibrant feelings anew,
Soaring and gliding across the skies
Like operatic arias touching your core.
In fact you are so moved and ecstatic
You feel a need to beg for more.

So mesmerised by a dazzling light
That seems to shine right inside,
Your very secret, inner soul
Leaving nowhere left to hide.
For like a melting of frozen lakes
Washing all the icebergs away,
A controlling spirit leads you
To another rapturous day.

Thus stunned and filled with wonder
You walk majestically about,
Believing whatever comes now
Will be joyous without a doubt.
For slowly you come to realise
Some great miracle has occurred,
Brought by this faultless muse
That your whole being has stirred.

So who is this magnificent angel
And how did they spread such love?
For you now believe you're flying
Alongside passing clouds above.
The sun is now in your pocket
With many other exhilarations.
As you have come to realise
You're caught by loves sensations.

--ooOoo--

Desert

A desert with its vast distances
Of desolation and lonely quiet.
Would seem to many undesirable,
But for me and you just right.
For I could have you all to myself
So not have to worry about others,
Who could perhaps discover us
And maybe blow our covers.

But I have special plans for you
My stunning and beautiful queen,
Who has put this magic spell on me
That I'd never before felt or seen.
So therefore I must act now
As you would desire me do,
Though I am finding it easier
For I have put my spell on you.

Thus together in our own desert
And alone beneath a sky of stars,
I can take you on ecstatic journeys
Soaring across both Jupiter and Mars,
Before fluttering back all a quiver
Across your entire being and soul.
For our desolate loving motions
Have made our bodies whole.

So indulge this sand-less desert
That will always be our own,
With you in captivating wonder
As you see how I have grown,
In my total devotion to you
When we are joined by all parts.
That gives constant bliss to make
Just one from our two hearts.

--ooOoo--

Flutter

When I catch your lovely smile
I flutter deep inside me,
And with those twinkling eyes
I am now all lost at sea.

But please don't stop that smile
Or let your eyes lose their shine,
For at my very lowest moments
They appear to me so fine,
With a never ending story
Beamed out from your face,
To make me flutter more
And send me to outer space.

For it doesn't take too much
To make all our hearts flutter,
And we can zoom into orbit
From the quietest little mutter,
That you feel the same as me
And that my look is the very best.
So how can we possibly lose
When much better than the rest?

So move on from smiley twinkling
Of your mouth and shining eyes,
To touch me in your special way
Which causes no great surprise,

That I only flutter with you
As you've seen me melt away,
Wanting to hear, and see you
Every minute of each day!

--ooOoo--

Sleepwalking

Sleepwalking is both a combination
Of deep sleep and being awake,
When unknown and without intent
You can make your big mistake.
For this can occur during sleep
Repeating things done when alert,
Possibly sitting up or talking aloud
And actions likely to hurt.

But far more serious than this
Is if engaged in complex tasks.
Such as cooking or even driving
You start before anyone asks,
If you are feeling alright and sure
That you are able to safely do,
Such things when looking drowsy
Causing harm to others or you.

Though of course you may not recall
Such experiences of potential harm.
Whilst sleepwalking oblivious,
If causing people alarm.

But possibly another explanation
Perhaps more personal to me,
As I ghost about and all around
Trying so desperately to see,
My spiritual long lost muse
Who had sent me all her love,
Before sadly being taken away
And maybe sent to live above.

--ooOoo--

Shiver

If our bodies feel cold we shiver
Or perhaps have a nervous thought,
Because our systems are very sensitive
And emotive reactions can be caught.
So knowing cold weather can affect us
We need to always wrap up warm,
To protect ourselves from feeling
Any draft from an icy storm.

We must also try hard to guard
Against those moments of unease,
If discomfort or fearful reactions
Our nerve ends they don't please,
Such as in those stressful situations
That make our body feel a strain,
Which our learning process teaches
Not to get into again.

But there is another kind of shiver
And that is one of pure delight,
Which comes over me completely
If I kiss or hold you tight.
Especially when you tell me
You are having nice shivers too,
That you say is all down to me
And the little things I do.

Which of course brings us alive
And makes our heartbeats sing,
So we then welcome those shivers
And all the ecstasy they bring.

--ooOoo--

Close

Close is an intimate nearness
Of two bodies tight together.
And when that's me with you
I don't think that I could ever
Consider the heartache and pain
Of ever being torn apart,
From all your warm soft contours
Or the kindness of your heart.

So allow me to snuggle up
And encompass us both and hold
You in my passionate embrace
That all inhibitions will unfold.
Leading to those sensations
From pulsing of passions flame,
Sparked off by our desires
We must release without shame.

With our lips exploring secrets
And wonders that they find,
Amongst the sensual closeness
Of the intense lovers grind.
Following all those emotions
That a close bonding feeds,
Until volcanic movements cease
With the conclusion of our needs.

For now we have uncovered
The secrets of close touch,
So will practice continually
For we can never have too much.

--ooOoo--

Bears in Love

Ted and Beth have been together
For over thirteen years now,
And still they love one another
Both uttering a teddy "wow",
When they smile and have a cuddle
That they will frequently do.
For though they often muck about
Their love for each other is true.

Beth was alone when found by Ted
And since they've never been apart,
Being a very true loving pair
Joined by a special teddy heart.

They have also shared adventures
Like touring Australia in a tent,
And going off on a long cruise
They thought was heaven sent.
Now regularly going to France
They'll relax at their place there,
Enjoying a dinghy on the lake
And playing without a care.

Though they find time for mischief
Getting up to naughty japes,
As they're both still young at heart
Constantly getting into scrapes.

But mostly the bears love each other
Although fame has brought temptation,
But their regard for life together
Won't allow a tarnished reputation.
So they continue as a perfect couple
Happily sharing time and joy,
Because Beth is Ted's special lady
And he's her favourite teddy boy.

--ooOoo--

Daisy

Now Daisy Bear is quite attractive
And wears a very pretty dress,
But when found in a charity shop
She was in a state of great distress,
Which calmed as I picked her up
But with regret put her back down,
As I was worried about having room
Which made her sad and frown.

Though I was much taken with her
And the manager used her voice,
To try and persuade me to take her
Making it a very difficult choice.
Although knowing if I did take her
It will be against my own advice.
A deal was done though for Daisy,
When the shop dropped the price.

So she happily came home with me
To meet a rapidly growing group,
Of bears and friends sitting about
With one or two needing to stoop,
To fit in the diminishing space
Where they all love to meet.
So I really cannot buy any more
And see a lack of room defeat.

Though Daisy shows her gratitude
Of being rescued from that store,
And says being cramped in a box
Made her uncomfortable and sore.
So now Daisy has easily settled in
And Beth and her are great friends,
Which makes me feel very happy
As they enjoy all carefree trends.

Praising Naughty Girls

So called naughty girls get bad press
But what defines a naughty girl,
Is she one who leads men astray
Or gets them dizzy and in a whirl?
For I don't think this can be right
As many women are just like that,
So maybe it is just their defence
When men come on with their chat.

No, I think that this naughty girl
Is meant to be a lady too free,
With her favours and charms
To woo the likes of little ol' me?
But just hang on here a bit
As I don't think this is very fair,
Because in my experience with ladies
They're much the same everywhere.

Well very similar that is to men
And who seem to escape much flak,
When spreading oats and seeds
So why slate women who do it back?
Oh yes this is quite a conundrum
For upstanding society pillars to take,
Because if they look at themselves
They are the same for goodness sake!

So give me please a naughty girl
That I can easily get to know,
And if my knowledge doesn't reach
She will be only too eager to show
Me all the great pleasures for her,
That she will then return back for me.
And there is nothing wrong with that
So leave these naughty girls be.

--ooOoo--

One Voice

I woke to the disappointment
Of rain hammering my mobile home,
For a storm seemed right overhead
And was pounding the roof dome.
So I turned over and back to sleep
To awake again in another hour,
But sadly the rain had not ceased
And thus my mood was sour.

But laying in bed hearing the din
A minor miracle then occurred,
For against the noise on my roof
Came the sweet singing of a bird.
A solitary chirping of morning joy
From a little chap I couldn't see,
But the song he continually sang
Was a great delight to me.

Though what had motivated this bird
Whose song beat the noisy rain,
I'm sure I will never really know
But he kept up with his refrain.
Now I'm no great bird expert
So couldn't tell the type or family,
But because he sang out in a storm
His form I didn't need to see.

For soon a couple of other birds
Joined in with the singular voice,
Maybe encouraged and led by him
Or perhaps just their own choice.

So now against a strong backdrop
Of rain clattering on my roof,
I had this wonderful little choir
Singing out in beautiful proof,
That even in our dismal times
A determined song by one voice,
Can overcome depressive scenes
To offer a happier choice.

--ooOoo--

Cut Loose

It may take time before you feel
The endings of your strife
And trembling release of pent up needs,
Freeing frustrations from your life.

So gasping from all the excitement
Brand new excursions can bring,
You will lay down breathless
Whilst heartbeat joys still sing,
Of skin touches, that made you gasp
And brought sleeping nerves alive.
Ensuring that your desired vibes
Would all very soon arrive.

But why were you so lost in sleep
That you took so long to wake?
Perhaps you were just not aware
Of sacrifices you must make.
For nothing comes from nothing
Unless you determine now to try,
To let all those trapped emotions go
Released with ecstatic sigh.

So relax and welcome sensations
Exploding in body and mind,
That maybe never reached the heights
Of these vibrant present kind,
That overcame the long journey
To climb to the very top.
And knowing that if you allow,
They may never, ever stop!

--ooOoo--

Mary Go Round

Sandra fancies the pants off Dave
But he only has eyes for Mary,
Which is pretty unfortunate really
As she wants to be Andy's fairy.

But Sandra is a very determined girl
So will flash her eyes at Dave,
And so each opportunity she has
Will try to attract him and wave,
Of course ensuring her top is low
And that her skirt is very short,
But whilst Dave quite likes the view
He has no intention of being caught.

Well that is by the sexy Sandra
As he is quite aware of her game,
But Dave's amorous eyes are for Mary
And poor Sandra's just not the same.
For he is trying very hard to impress
Mary as his much desired girl,
But meanwhile Dave is unaware
That Mary wants Andy in this whirl.

Maybe best to have a little re cap
Of exactly who fancies who,
So we have Sandra wanting Dave
Who likes Mary, but she wants Andy to
Be hers, so she flutters and wiggles,
At Andy whenever he's around.
But of course he is totally oblivious
He is on loves dangerous ground.

So all have their desires frustrated
Like many love dreams can do,
For as these folks fancy one another
Our Andy has set his sights on Sue,
That has really upset poor Mary
Which Dave just can't quite work out,
So poor Sandra is also disappointed
In this failed love roundabout.

--ooOoo--

Gratitude

Thank you mum and dad
For the gifts you bestowed on me,
I'm just sorry it took me so long
The very depth of them to see.

You taught me to count my blessings
Although we were always poor,
But love and happiness prevailed
Of that I was certainly sure.
And though you were not young
At the time that I was born,
You did everything for, and with me
So I could never be forlorn.

I'm told I wasn't always easy
And could play up like a clown,
But you never worried much
Saying that I would soon calm down.

Mum was taken at only seventy three
Though dad had a much longer life,
Which was quite amazing really
After childhood poverty and strife.

But they had a smiling effervescence
Which carried us across life's woe,
Thus again I will thank you for this
As it follows wherever I go.

I wish I could talk to you now
To say thanks again for all your care,
And perhaps reflect you would be proud
Of my achievements I want to share.
Like my degree and career I had
That may have been beyond your view,
And now a six times published poet
That I know is all down to you.

So I say to you many thanks again
For the characteristic traits you gave,
That ensure I will be smiling always
Until I'm put down in my grave.

--ooOoo--

Royal George

George is a new teddy in the family
And he has a sort of regal bearing,
When he surveys his new environment
And at his surroundings he is staring.

But if at first he seems a bit severe
When he glances across at you,
It is more of his look of interest
When he watches what you do.
Because he has great compassion
And tremendous love of being alive,
For now he has some new friends
His life interests will all thrive.

Although we don't know too much
Of the regal George's early years,
Though I detect a hint of sadness
And maybe a few shed teddy tears.
But now he has his new family
To talk to, and play with him,
Who will also give much respect
And not allow him to look grim.

So if he appears to lean forward
As if was a bit hard of hearing,
You could maybe be mistaken
If you thought that he was leering.
But that is not the case at all
As he's a clever and caring bear,
So just relax and cherish him
And his unusual loving stare.

--ooOoo--

Loves Illusion Confusion

The enigma of our emotions
Can reduce the vision of our eyes,
To cause misconception of images,
And make us victims of any lies.

For when love and attractions call
Important messages can be missed,
With all the alarm bells ringing
From that moment you are kissed
By your hopeful dream time figure,
Who for you may not be quite right.
But with emotional blinkers on now
You may not have perfect sight.

Because love lines and heartstrings
Don't always listen to our brain,
When attractive compliments play
Ensuring decisions aren't always sane.
But an overwhelmed and lovestruck
Heart and soul can be fooled,
Into uncharted feelings and waters
Maybe regretted if love has cooled.

Though enjoy those precious moments
For they might not come again to you,
And what other people think or say
May not always be genuine or true.
So let any recriminations come later
If some concerns are in your head,
As one thing is for certain sure
You can't love her when you're dead.

--ooOoo--

Ted n Beth at Prayer

We must now hush and be silent
Making no disturbance or move,
For Ted and Beth are at prayer
Their consciences trying to smooth.

Like Christopher Robin in his story
When no one whispers or dares,
To interrupt a boy, or bears now
As they offer up their prayers.
Those teddy legs bent in tribute
And holding together their paws,
This is exactly how I found them
In this reverent pose indoors.

With both pairs of eyes closed
To keep worldly distractions out,
Our bears seek some forgiveness
For their noise and mucking about,
And making domestic disruption
Which to them is a great laugh.
Like when they went much too far
And overflowed their bath!

But Ted and Beth will continue
In their most mischievous ways,
Because they are both rarely quiet
Causing chaos on most days.

So although they don't want to stop
They do realise they are naughty.
Which gave them this idea
Of a little prayer offering sortie,
To close those little teddy eyes
And offer up a contrite refrain.
But knowing in their hearts
They will just be naughty again.

--ooOoo--

Hypnotic Dance

Everyone has a love song
Or poem deep in their heart,
Maybe you can never sing it
But knowing it is a start,
To begin to seek your dream
Of a love you never found.
So you slowly start to move
Towards that luring sound.

Hypnotic rhythms stealing thoughts
When drawn forward in a trance,
To the person of your desires
Who is wanting you to dance,
While cuddling up so tight
Before kissing that loving face
You now know waits for you,
At that magic, sensual place.

So with bated breathe and hope
That was never there before,
You prepare to meet your muse
Of which you're really sure.
Because this love song tells you
Something great is coming,
And while you wait and tremble
Loves music is now strumming.

Therefore you sway and wallow
In loves mood that's oh so deep,
Without the slightest movement
To awake you from your sleep!

--ooOoo--

Frozen

Anything frozen can be chilled or cold
Into a state of freshness preserved,
So in a manner of speaking then
Just like something you've reserved,
To come back to when appropriate
And usually this will be your food.
But in other types of occasions
Maybe an event to be pursued.

Now that can be very convenient
As life does not always suit,
The situation or circumstance
On your current travel route,
Which could not work out exactly
As you would much prefer it to.
So leaving it for sometime later
Is more appealing to you.

So I guess that is my situation
As I now return your way,
For I had frozen my feelings
Seeming like forever and a day.

But now all the boxes are ticked
And the timing feels just right,
For me to come and sweep you
Off your feet and out of sight.
As my frozen state was melting
I did not feel I could hold on,
Too much longer to find you
And my moment might be gone.

But I can see now by your face
You still have me in your heart,
As I swoop to lovingly take you
Where will never be apart.

--ooOoo--

Desired Effect

In your dreams and imagination
You can conjure perfect sight.
So fashioned just for you,
It's sure to fit you right
Up your street and in your door,
As if by magic it arrived,
Delivered just for you
To ensure your wish survived!

Fantasies and pictured visions
You would like to have with you,
Can be brought to walk along
Just as if they were all true.
For the powers of want and need
May fan desires into flame,
So wish for your sensations
Without a hint of shame!

Thus have no fear of calling
Unseen icons to your mind,
Perhaps of people not yet met
Who would be nice to find.
For inside our rampant brain
Our ideas can ebb and flow,
Allowing all perceptions in
To where you want to go!

--ooOoo--

HUMOUR

No Hiding Place

At our local swimming pool
You can see many a curious sight.
With lots of lovely young girls,
Whilst other scenes are a fright.

Men wearing tight fitting trunks,
"Budgie Smugglers" for the thin.
Though sadly worn by some "largies"
Having more hanging out, than in!
For it seems a life contradiction
That the larger many folk grow,
Instead of tucking it safely away
They must put it all out on show.

Now I'm not against big sizes
I have a growing waist myself,
But I fervently try to hide it
Not put it on the front shelf.

But back to those swimming trunks
Of varying size of modesty cover,
With the battle of those bulges
Where some really need another
Or much larger piece of cloth,
To keep their harvest all intact.
For hiding mountains behind a stamp
Won't work, and that's a fact!

--ooOoo--

Humpty Dumpty Revisited

Most people know about Humpty Dumpty
But how many know the story facts?
And maybe wonder why he sat on a wall
With a shell that so easily cracks.
And was it partly his obese type figure
That rendered him in danger to fall,
For surely he should have thought
He might easily slip off the wall?

And then the involvement of kings men
Who were presumably meant to guard,
And not fuss over an accident prone egg
So perhaps they didn't try too hard
To put his pieces back together again,
And cleaned up helped by their horse.
Who really had no choice in all this,
But then you guessed that of course?

Now onto the popularity of Humpty
Among the townsfolk needing to beg,
For food, money and other problems
And no time to worry over an egg,
Who apparently never did much work
Perhaps explaining why he was fat.
Because we need exercise and labour
And not just sit on a wall like that!

So on thinking about what happened
To cause him being put back together,
After his famous "egg stravigant" fall
Which really wasn't that clever.
For the working folk of the kingdom
Are all really now tired and bushed,
So that brings me to the conclusion
The unpopular Humpty was pushed!

--ooOoo--

Up or Down?

There is a monumental dilemma
Which can make us smile or frown.
For it concerns the toilet seat
And should we leave it up or down?

Now this debate has run for years
And driven men and women apart,
Because there is no neutral ground
As opinions come from the heart.
For men will often lift the seat
But then neglect to put it back,
Which of course infuriates ladies,
So they will come out and attack.

But men say that they lift the seat
In an act of common courtesy,
As they don't want to be accused
Of spraying little drops of wee,
For not lifting up the toilet seat
Could risk it getting a trifle wet.
So if that's the unpleasant case
A damp bum is what you get.

Though ladies will argue their case
Of men's behaviour not being right,
And accuse them of being careless
If leaving the loo a messy sight.
For women continually say to men
That they need to try much more,
Not to leave seats up and damp
Or sprinkle on the floor.

Thus the argument still continues
And has done so much too long,
But I feel if leaving the seat down,
Men will still be in the wrong.
For it seems that there's no answer
Even if you fully use your wit,
But perhaps men should try harder
So women smile as they sit.

--ooOoo--

Diddler on the Roof

I could hear a sort of banging
That was to turn out exactly right,
But nothing causing the noise
Was at that point in my sight.

It seemed to come from next door
So for my neighbour I was concerned,
But any possible noise of her banging
Had many years ago been spurned.
So did she have workmen in
Knocking her fixtures all about?
Though on checking she was safe
I confirmed that she was out.

So this racket I couldn't ignore
Clearly came from another direction,
And was really beginning to bug me
Thus called for a closer inspection,
Of all around my own property
And so I looked about outside.
To be confronted by some seagulls
Making love with a fervent pride!

Therefore it really was a banging
Causing all the noisy din,
But gulls don't know the saying
About being better out than in.

For whatever the male was doing
To make his seagull lady squeak,
It was involved and very lively
All out action with his beak.

Now I'm really not a spoilsport
And everyone shows loving proof,
Of how they feel for their partner
But not on my bloody roof!

So showing my authority now
And that I could also bang,
I shut my garden box loudly
With a deep resounding clang,
To stop further amorous activity
And all their romantic sorties,
Which hopefully would then deter
Any future loud sexy naughties.

For if they want to continue now
They must do so without fuss,
Or I will soon be teaching them
All about coitus interrupt us!

--ooOoo--

Bell End

I loved my football from an early age
And began to regularly go to matches,
Though being small and young in years
Often watched the games in snatches.
For in big crowds it was hard to see
Though you might be let down the front,
So I mostly got a good view
Amongst the crowds push and shunt.

Now I don't recall actually when
That I decided to get a bell,
Which I bought down the market
And it would raise devils in their hell.
Some people would have a rattle
Which made a clanking sound,
But I'm sure that Laurie's bell
Was heard all across the ground.

So I felt quite chuffed with this
Though I had begun to realise,
It wasn't popular with everyone
Because of its ring, and not the size,
Which wasn't that particularly big
But the clang was really loud.
Again not pleasing all about me,
Though I felt very proud.

The trouble, and the bells demise
Came about when we scored a goal,
In a very close, important game
So I rang out heart and soul.
But tragically I went too mad
And hit a big bloke in the face,
Who wasn't pleased and threatened
To put my bell up a personal place.

Thus that really spelt the sad end
Of me taking my bell with me,
As the crowd were mostly regulars
So the same people I would see.

Which invoked prudence over courage
Although I did think about a drum,
But I worried if I got one of those
The bloke might shove it up my bum.
So I decided to just shout out loud
Like others, who would also sing.
And though I still enjoyed myself
I really missed my bell to ring!

--ooOoo--

Ladies Wait and Queue

We must all attend the lavatory,
Something men and women must do.
Though it seems unfair at times
As mostly only women queue.

For biological make up of our bodies
Ensure that both gender goes,
To the toilet every now and then,
But as ladies sit men can go in rows.
Which is obviously much quicker
As they don't need to close a door.
So the only concern that we have
Is not to dribble on the floor.

Obviously there are times that men
Need to sit down to perform as well,
And I have to admit on occasions
Some men seem to sleep, or dwell,
During this seated occupation,
But happily we mostly just stand.
As ladies have to wait patiently
When queue's get out of hand.

Therefore we humble men appreciate
Personal attributes we have got,
That allows us to tinkle easily
While ladies need to squat.
Though of course in a shared toilet
Men must determine to be neat.
So must not sprinkle carelessly,
And to always lower the seat!

So this is one of life's differences
Of behaviours going to the loo,
Thus men can smugly just continue
While ladies must wait and queue.

--ooOoo--

Bears New Friend Tigger

I've just got a new family guest
And he could barely be much bigger,
When he joins the teddy family
And comes bouncing up as Tigger.
Yes "Winnie the Pooh's" old friend
Well they were most of the time,
But Tigger could be a right pest
And upset the peace sublime.

Then why have I bought this tiger
As nearly all the family are bears?
I guess I just wanted a change,
Although nobody really cares
When I introduce my accomplices
To residency or care homes in sight,
For they are always well received
Often giving great delight.

So I must admit I was too tempted
And probably didn't stop to figure,
Where he would sit or even fit in
The day I bought big bouncy Tigger.
But not to worry it's done now
And all the bears seem to like him,
So he fits in pretty well at home
Because he's quite tall and slim.

So anyway he has joined us all
And I don't want to hear any snigger,
Because I'm a poet with teddy bears
Who has now also bought a Tigger.
For I think that he suits me nicely
Reading my poems out for you.
So I had to write this new verse,
To say why I now have a tiger too.

Now it's accepted Tigger is part of
My growing teddy bear family true,
Nearly always making folks smile
When we come to meet all of you,
Interesting and wonderful folks
Who seem to enjoy poems I say.
So that's also a pleasure for me,
As we enjoy another nice day

--ooOoo--

Leggings Don't Tell Lies

There are many varied clothing items
For men and women, large and small,
But these can be fraught with danger
For some you shouldn't wear at all.

Well that is if you are larger
And maybe ate too many pies,
So be careful with what you choose ,
For those leggings don't tell lies.
Because they're invariably tight fitting
And not so easy to get over thighs,
Giving a too-small-for-you picture
As those leggings won't tell lies.

For even if you pull them high
Over your legs and up your belly,
There is not any hiding places
So your middle shakes like a jelly.
And anyway I just can't work it out
If you have a fuller figure size,
Why people won't get extra large
Because leggings don't tell lies.

So on and on the struggle goes
Just like the battle of the bulge,
But by wearing those tight leggings
All your large areas you divulge.

For if you must wear figure hugging
It's far better that you get wise,
And don't go near tight britches
Because leggings don't tell lies.

Though of course we all like to try
Various fashions that catch our eyes,
And it is very easy to get caught
So remember leggings won't tell lies.

But please don't despair too much
If your body is large with flaws,
Go ahead and wear what you want,
But probably best you stay indoors!

--ooOoo--

Fly Past

Flying creatures can be aggravating
And get you extremely mad,
Buzzing around and landing on food
Like an airborne "Jack the Lad".

Some can give you a sting as well
Filling many folks with dread,
That they will get a nasty prick
As they zoom around their head.
But flapping your arms all about
Won't work and can make you grieve,
For you will get stung for sure
If you trap one up your sleeve.

But what is it about those little flies
That makes us lose our wit?
Perhaps it's because they like poo
With a passion to roll in it,
And then eat some for a meal
For that's exactly what they do,
Ensuring that when they land on us
It can make us want to spew.

Though one special annoying thing
Is that persistent little fly,
Who however many times you swat
Just determines not to die.
So you flail your hands manically
Trying to give it a fatal crack,
But when you think you've got him
The blighter comes flying back.

So the war on this tiny air force
Can go to extreme lengths,
Although it's a very unequal fight
With very different strengths.
For you do your level best to kill
Your miniature battling foe,
Who when you think that you've won
Will do a fly past, and then go!

--ooOoo--

Five Limericks

1

Now the lovely Helen of Troy
Fell in love with a pretty young boy,
But on getting down to the act
It became a sad fact,
That he could give her no joy!

2

A very fat dancer from Rheims
Would eat to pig-like extremes,
So her increasing size
Was a feast for your eyes,
As her costume split at the seams.

3

There was a tom cat from Kent
Who was rude to such an extent,
That he pooed in my garden
But never said pardon,
So over the wall he went.

4

There was a lady from Pinner
Who had a desire to be thinner,
So on a strict diet she went
And with her yoga moves bent,
Showing all she'd had for dinner.

5

An old hippy having a trip
Let his hair grow past his hip,
But though he wants peace
He also needs grease,
To free his hair from his zip.

--ooOoo--

Double Vision

I went into this village pub
For I was dying for a beer,
But I was very soon to learn
Not to ever come in here.

For I stood at the bar patiently
With a throat dry as a bone,
Despite coughing and shuffling
It seemed I was all alone.

But then a noise behind the bar
Caught both my ear and attention,
And with a very surprised eye
Saw the cause of service retention.
For the Landlady and barman both,
Were doing what comes naturally,
So I realised to my dismay
Neither would be serving me!

Now in a huff I went round the side
And into the other bar,
But saw a barmaid and Landlord
In a clinch that went too far.

So storming out for another pub
That would hopefully quench a thirst,
I tripped over two copulating dogs
And furiously upon them burst,
With barely contained fury now
Complete with an angry frown,
I threw the randy dogs inside
Saying your ruddy sign fell down!

--ooOoo--

Ellie Elephant

Ellie elephant is big and strong
As I suppose that she should be,
But obviously our Ellie isn't real
Though has likenesses you can see,
Put into her cuddly animal frame
That attracts all love and caring,
With a pair of big bright eyes
You could mistake as staring.

But Ellie is a very peaceful copy
Of a huge elephant specimen
That's one of our largest creatures,
Mostly benign and gentle when
They are left to their own devices,
Wandering about natural habitat.
But they can be quite ferocious
If provoked or anything like that.

So back to our domestic Ellie
Rescued from a shop for charity,
When I spotted her friendly look
And so took her home with me.

Well actually it wasn't that simple
For Ellie is solid with a long hooter.
And being unable to fit her inside it
Rode with me on my motor scooter.

Which I think she really enjoyed
For she trumpeted in a happy way,
As we rode carefully back home
So I think I had made her day.

Now the bears and friends family
Hadn't really seen her like before,
And all soon made friends with her
So they'll happy together I'm sure,
Taking it in turns to come with me
When I go to read my poems out,
At various fundraising events
Causing joy without a doubt

--ooOoo--

I Wish I Could Whistle

I wish that I could whistle
Even if it wasn't quite in tune,
For when I purse my lips and blow
My cheeks swell like a balloon.

I used to be able to whistle a bit
Although in truth it was not great,
But I happily just blasted away
Until threatened with a fate
That was quite nasty and hostile
If I didn't stop my whistle shrill.
Which to me was disappointing
And like a very bitter pill!

For my dad was a terrific whistler
And could yodel properly too,
But my attempts were pretty sad
No matter what I tried to do.
So when I heard people sound
Their whistle heard near a mile,
I must admit to feeling envious
About my efforts so futile.

I watched people put two fingers
Past their lips and in the mouth,
And emit a screeching sound
That travelled north and south.

While others made less effort
For a shrill success as well,
But all my lip pursing efforts
Made my tongue hurt like hell.

So I could never be a wolf
Who whistled at girls passing by.
Though frowned on now to do that,
But I couldn't even try!

Thus I have given it up now
And will no longer try to blast,
My sound through lips and teeth
To come out slow or fast,
Or in fact make much of a noise
Leaving no doubts of my epistle,
That whilst not a bad bloke in life
He could never, ever whistle.

--ooOoo--

Circus

I'm not a lover of the Big Top
With the contrived acts in the ring,
For I much prefer the circus of life
And the entertainment that will bring.
Which of course is what I write on
From observations of animal tamers,
Trapeze artists and those clowns
Just like many real world gamers.

Then there has to be a ring master
In charge of Big Top antics too,
Just like big shots in our lives
Wanting to boss about me and you.

But by far of greatest interest
To sardonic views of your world,
Are people and strange behaviours
Not knowing they are unfurled.

Because the funniest of clowns
Are people wanting to be revered,
Though it doesn't quite come off
When from respect they steered.
And so many other circus like acts
Performed by buffoons in life,
Trying to show off, or juggle things
Which only leads to their strife.

Some people wanting to control
As an animal tamer of the house,
Which all falls sadly flat for them
For they're mostly like a mouse,
That creeps quietly about and hides
So it doesn't get found or seen,
Because for them any bravado act
Isn't exactly what they mean.

There are also those other folks
Doing their somersaults for us,
But after exertions and endeavours
Nothing shows for all their fuss.

So perhaps just accept that a circus
Is best left to the performers way,
Because how ever hard some try
They will still be clowns each day.

--ooOoo--

Naked Ambition

The shower setting at the gym
Is a place for communal undress,
With all kinds of behaviour
But perhaps some you should guess.

You can see all the different types
By their various mannerisms there.
For some are quite shy and bashful,
But others just stand and stare!

There is though one unwritten code
Whether you smile or wear a frown.
It says you can do much as you like
But you never ever look down.

Though some it doesn't seem to faze
They swagger like a smiling punk.
I'm sure it wouldn't matter to them,
If they had a finger, or a trunk!

Others creep quickly out the shower,
A private person you'd have guessed.
It's possible that they're very quiet
Or else not been well blessed.

The kingpin though, a man of brawn
Absolute content with what he's got.
But catching a glance in a mirror
It was surprisingly not a lot!

As for me with my large sized mouth,
I'm just happy to laugh with those.
Who also have no reason to brag,
But you'd not like it on your nose!

--ooOoo--

Big Bruno

Bruno is a really big teddy bear
And I do mean quite a size,
So when I eventually got him home
I wondered if I had been wise?

But before we even get round to that
I had decided to take a chance,
As I removed him from his sad corner
Where he had scarcely had a glance,
Perhaps because he was so big
So wouldn't just tuck nicely away.
And he certainly needs a lot of room
With nothing else you can say.

Though after paying for Big Bruno,
You see he already had his name,
I had to think quickly on my feet
And play a sort of children's game.
For I didn't want to leave Bruno
But needed to go shopping in Tesco,
Which meant I had to take him
And in the only place he could go.

So I sat him boldly in the front
Of my Tesco supermarket trolley,
And wheeled him all around the shop
Without really feeling a walley,

Because most people smiled at me
Or was it more at my giant Ted?
I can't tell you the answer to that,
As nothing much was said.

Although of course, me being me
I did explain Big Bruno was a "prop",
Who I would take to poetry gigs
Knowing he would never be a flop.
For he would come with Ted and Beth
Now very much two celebrity bears,
And popular with all our audiences
With many appreciative stares.

Thus eventually we got to go home
So Bruno met his new found friends,
Who were all delighted to see him
Hoping their happiness never ends,
For Big Bruno fills an important role
To be Ted and Beth's bodyguard,
Keeping them both safe and sound
And remain in high regard.

So eventually the excitement ended
And all the bears soon settled down,
Confident they'll be looked after well
Never having to wear a frown.

--ooOoo--

Neill at the Bar

Neill is the steward at the "Boro Club"
So you can always see him around,
And he normally is quite affable
Unless you give pennies for a pound,
For he worries he might drop those
So you may be short for your sup.
But a much bigger problem for Neill
Is bending down to pick them up.

Also beware of his sardonic humour
Which sneaks out behind his smile,
Coming briefly before his one liner
Delivered in just that little while,
After he has heard your comment
So allows a gap before his crack,
To ensure that he is again ready
If you dare to answer back.

But don't be misled by his inertia
As he sits ready at the bar table,
For he will casually observe all
Of his parish, so is quite able,
To resolve any query or a need
In his efforts to make all good,
Any new incident now occurring
Just as a Bar Steward should.

So it could be easy to be fooled
Neill is totally cynical and not care,
But behind that time-served grin
A considerate heart is beating there,
For he carefully monitors his flock
To see if there's any need or support,
He can resolve a bit, or help out
And bring their worries to a halt.

So Steward Neill is a sort of angel
Although these days his halo droops,
For he's seen most, but maybe forgotten
He might not look his best in hoops.
Although when affecting a rescue
Of anyone who has had too much,
He can be forgiven any flaws
Providing the Club's caring touch.

--ooOoo--

Sofa so Good

There are times to change your sofa
And splash out on that new settee,
So I am writing about it now
As it has just been done by me.

But it really isn't that simple
For they must be changed over too,
Getting rid of the old one first
Which can be a battle before you do,
Because what seemingly came in easy
May not go out quite the same,
As you have added shelves and carpets
But your old sofa can't remain.

For you have the new one coming
Which means you need the space,
Being taken up by the old one
So it is now a desperate race,
Though with just a little thought
And some extra care now spent,
You can get the old one removed
Thus no expletives are vent.

So with worthy paid for muscle
The exchange is successfully done,
Which means you use your new one
And that kicks off some more fun.
For where your "botty" happily sat
Over many a week and long year,
You must now wriggle and move
Towards perfect comfort cheer.

But finally it all goes very well
Just like a settee exchange should,
So you sit content and contemplate
That it's all sofa so good!

--ooOoo--

Handfight at the OK Sauce Table

Like the famous gunfight at OK corral
That was decided by superior force,
We can have our very own battle
If wanting to use the OK Sauce.

For their bottles can put up a fight
And be determined to frustrate you,
By refusing to serve smoothly
Whatever you try to do.
Because if the sauce is in there
It just won't come out the top.
Until you squeeze it in temper,
And then it just won't stop.

So you are faced with a meal
Covered with sauce now spread,
All over your waiting food
Which makes you lose your head,
And rant in a foul temper
In front of friends and those,
Who are now trying not to laugh
At your spattered plate and clothes.

Thus it may be time to withdraw
Or just quietly sit back down,
Gingerly trying to clear the mess
And attempt to smile, not frown.

Until a waiter comes to the rescue
As if summoned by a desperate bid,
Not to fall apart in embarrassment
When he calmly unscrews the lid,
Of the bottle you tried to squash
That didn't need squeezing at all.
For the bottle had a twist action,
So you're a sauce spattered fool!

--ooOoo--

The Lonely Life of a Lemon

The poor old lemon has a lonely life
Because it can never win it seems,
Despite adding taste to many drinks
As from the glass it gleams.

But very few own up to lemon liking
It is one of those unwritten laws,
For a lemon has some connotations
That are associated with dull bores,
Also it has quite a thick skin
With a very sour and acidic taste.
So being seen as, or called a lemon
Is not a great thing to be faced.

For anybody who is called a lemon
Is meant to be an unsatisfactory type
Or of defective or feeble nature,
Although that may be just the hype.
Because lemons do have their uses
In the culinary world and for cleaning,
So before writing the poor lemon off
You better check on its meaning.

For lemons are popular in cooking
And go to make lemon meringue pie,
Which is a favourite of many people
So can cause a glint in their eye.
And let's not forget the lemon curd
That is appreciated by folks too,
So it seems downsides of lemons
May not always be totally true.

Though of course we must understand
How the lemon can stand alone.
As it has quite a sour taste to it
So can mean people who like to moan,
As are often referred to as a lemon
Or thick skinned according to some.
But best beware of their acid side
As they may have a bite at your bum.

Thus the much maligned sad lemon
Hasn't really done too much wrong,
To cause it to be ostracised and lonely
And kept from the smiling throng.

--ooOoo--

Poet Reflects Your World

REFLECTION

Damsons and Distress

I was born and bred a "townie"
Although the countryside was near,
But I knew more of the market
Than a farms mysterious sphere.
So as I wandered about the streets
I was then blissfully unaware,
That many roads can cross in life
And to a farm and working there.

Now it wasn't like a proper job
Back in that seventies decade,
When a situation came to pass
And decisions had to be made.
For I was working in a factory
Caught in an industrial dispute,
So we went on a three day week
That our budgets didn't suit.

Now many of the hard up workers
Took to doing jobs that were new,
On many local farms and land
With nothing they wouldn't do.
Thus quite unfortunate for me
As I had to be one of the last,
To try and find some casual job
So most vacancies had passed.

Though I did find employment
But no mates about, just me,
As I set to work on a new role
Picking damsons from a tree.
Well actually trees not just the one
And you needed to pick a lot,
To get much pay for your efforts
At an unfamiliar working spot.

There were other new experiences
Like balancing over a ladder rung,
That I soon realised wasn't my forte
For winds blew and branches swung.
But I needed to get some money
So did my best to avoid any harm,
Picking, but not squashing damsons
As I worked down on the farm.

I did take my radio for music
Which broke boredom with the sound,
But rocking away too much at times
I feared I may fall and hit the ground.
Which all went on for a few weeks
Until at last the dispute was resolved,
And I could return to my normal job
Feeling both relieved and involved.

So it remains just an amusing story
In the chequered past of my living,
But not one I would want to repeat
As it was hard work and unforgiving,
Hanging out alone in damson trees
Collecting fruit for a weighing scale,
That totalled up all my daily reward
And mostly an unhappy tale.

Thus another lesson for me in life
On counting blessings far and near,
So no more damsons distress for me
For I pursued a much better career.

--ooOoo--

Inquisition

We are all subject to inquisitions
But not only Spanish is now tried,
For they happen in many places
And also most countries world wide.
Because it's a decreed instruction
For any customer service dwelling,
And only varies in its content
Dependent on what they're selling.

So your inquisition can easily start
If you decide to go and have a coffee,
"Black or white, drink in, or take away
And do you want it made frothy?"
You flinch at all the questions asked,
And "was that small, medium or large?"
But the answers are quite important
As they will all affect the charge.

Now I know the world is complex
And few products remain the same,
But the numbers of varieties and diet
Make our requests a tricky game.

Many things can be confusing too
When confronted with so much choice,
"Brown or white, hot or cold is it?"
Though by now you've lost your voice,
Battered down by questioning spiel
They must practice in their sleep,
But to us poor bewildered customers
It is enough to make us weep.

Of course I understand it's progress
And a major desire to get things right,
But when you go to the counter now
You are verbally assailed on sight.
With even a simple water request
You get "will that be still or fizzy?"
And whilst I appreciate good service,
These inquisitions make me dizzy!

--ooOoo--

The Man Who Has Seen Everything

As we live on through our years
There is much that we can see,
Displayed by different experiences
In a vast world for you and me.
Although some people must keep safe
With a nervous concern of exploring,
So while they see all their little world
For others that is too boring.

Which then brings us to the bold
That want to embrace life with a gasp,
As adventures and new behaviours
Come happily within in their grasp.
Now I like to count myself in these
As I've not left many stones unturned,
Which opened up exciting routes
Thus for very little have I yearned.

So now I can say with an honesty
There isn't too much of life I've missed,
Such as cultures, behaviours and women
And quite a few of those I've kissed,
Which gives me a contented balance
To make me smile and my heart sing,
But our experiences must be tempered
Unlike the man who's seen everything.

For he has blinkered observations
And believes that he knows it all,
So as time had advanced with him
He became nervous and scared to fall,
Should he venture from his comfort zone
Now limited to narrow and addicted.
For he only has sheltered world
So to a miniscule life he's restricted.

But obviously he has to rationalise
And says no excitement is needed,
Because he really is now introvert
With perimeters that have receded,
To an almost hermit like existence,
Hiding in a world not big, but small.
For if he is approached or invited out
He fearfully says he's seen it all.

--ooOoo--

It's Agony

It never fails to amuse and perplex
Why people write to an agony aunt,
Because when it comes to giving advice
In the majority of cases they can't.

Now don't get me wrong about talking
Well if that's what a newspaper reply is,
For most of the problems are obvious
Like relationship advice for "Lonely Liz",
Who clearly has no basic understanding
Of peoples everyday ups and downs,
So while attempting to meet Mister Right,
Will surely only meet more clowns.

But back to the agony aunts spraying
Their advice on subjects large and small.
When it can clearly be seen they don't,
Have qualifications or knowledge at all.
For one has a family that's always arguing
About money, fame and what they say.
Whilst her life is not just a car crash,
More a giant pile up on the motorway.

Although to be fair they can only work
With the ludicrous problems sent,
A women compromised with a neighbour
Is asking why her husband went?

Other problems are also quite clear
Like a man who gets drunk and fights,
And that his wife won't give him sex
Though he tells her about his rights.
While other so called problems seen
Come from women and need little debate,
Because they over eat and binge drink
And ask why they put on weight.

Another gem that needs no professor
Is heavy smokers losing their breath.
Then ask is it cigarettes doing this,
And will it bring on early death?

Thus on it goes with our agony aunt
Prescribing answers and clearly not fit.
So my advice to their questioning folk
Is to not ask them, but Google it!

--ooOoo--

A Grain of Sand

A grain of sand, or a drop in the ocean
May be enough to cause commotion,
If brought together in one large amount
They can be big enough to make it count.
Because small or singles can be ignored
However many times they implored,
To get their point and views across
So are left staring at another loss.

For at most times in this cynical world
The tiny voice is lost until unfurled,
With the back up of a loud vast choir
That lift their voices so much higher,
And get all those points of view heard
With a collective singing of the word.
Just like the raging waters of a flood,
Which can harm both flesh and blood.

So be very wary of the seemingly small
Who could in years grow very tall,
And that little dog when just a pup
May really scare you when it grows up.
Thus one single grain of that fine sand
May have the ability to form a band,
Of determined people raising a voice
Into a storm that removes your choice.

Thus have a care before ignoring those
With a message and simple clothes,
As they may have the ability to dress
In uniform with others to bring distress,
That you may find very hard to take
When realising your big mistake,
In not seeing strength and mighty hand
Of drops of water and grains of sand!

--ooOoo--

Death of a Laptop

There are events in life we dread
Which make your heart nearly stop,
And one of those things for me
Is needing to replace my laptop.
Also changing my mobile phone
Will simply terrorise me as well.
As any upgrades of technology
Can bring on a certain hell.

For no matter all the assurances
That information will all be saved,
When you actually try to get it
You could easily become depraved.
As what is simple for the experts
Resolving problems so very quick,
Is not the exactly case for others
Who though bright are "techno thick".

Therefore to many various people
Another laptop or phone is dire,
So spend many a penny or prayer
Hoping their technology won't expire.
Because even if your favourite sites
Still remain on your new device,
Logging back in or finding them
Is rarely successful in a trice.

And when finding those places
On that device you often remain,
It is still not straightforward
For you to access them again.
So while mostly new laptops
Are much quicker than the last,
Which can be helpful at times
Until they conform too fast.

But all in all it is accomplished
With giant steps on technology way,
For we have to keep moving now
And no more that we can say,
To make us all feel better
Whether or not we try to hide,
As we make that dread discovery
That our laptop has just died.

--ooOoo--

I Can't Hear You

If you hurl abuse and ridicule
Which assail thick upon my ear,
Don't be surprised if I ignore you
As I'll turn deaf so just won't hear.
Thus if you wish to carry on
With slanders that aren't true.
Please note my sardonic smile,
As I really won't hear you.

For in life it is correctly said,
You please some people all the time.
And all the people just some of it,
Others may think your words a crime.
So everyone will have occasion
When people will criticise and abuse.
But I have a great remedy for this
As I only hear what I choose.

So don't allow others to bully you
Or dictate what you can say,
As people try to persuade you
To follow and think their way.
Of course it may seem the easiest
To just cave in and save the grief,
But stop to consider what they want
As may be lying through their teeth.

Thus I have now made a covenant
With my own integrity and pride,
As I don't want to be hijacked
So will have to run and hide.

Definitely better for you and me
That we stand up strong and true,
Because I won't hear the cheats
So they know what they can do!

--ooOoo--

The Bloke Down The Pub

Knowledge can come from anywhere
And encyclopaedias get to the nub,
But all this pales into insignificance
Compared to the bloke down the pub.
For he will have an answer to all
Perplexing dilemmas in our world,
And with just another sip of beer
His wisdom can be unfurled.

Finance, global warning or politics
Hold no fearful concern for him,
As he preaches all the solutions
Delivered at the merest whim
Or even a pause for breath,
Well maybe just another beer,
Before he continues to reiterate
His avid rhetoric so sincere.

Thus many an amateur DIY fan
Has joined the home disaster club,
After following the advice given
By that bloke down the pub.
Who also gives out his information
About solid investments so clear.
But when they all failed miserably
The pub bloke was nowhere near.

But technology, history or the law
Are all easy to the bloke at the bar,
Who assures all willing listeners
His knowledge can take them far,
Well perhaps this was partly true
If only in theory and not fact.
Because on most occasions
The correct answers he lacked.

So found in many insurance offices
And filed with a red alert stub,
Will be failed compensation claims
On advice given down the pub.

--ooOoo--

Cowboys and Motorists

In those days of the wild west
People all travelled around by horse,
Mostly riding on these animals
With coaches and carts of course.

So I wonder how it would all go
If we drove about like on horseback,
And substituted cars into that wild west
Maybe having to repel an Indian attack?
Would our vehicles cope with that terrain
Or lots of horses fit well in the city?
But I don't think we can ever see this
So in some ways that's a pity.

For many motorists driving behaviour
Lends itself to those lawless days,
Seen in the old western towns
Riding their horses in careless ways.

Though of course back in that rough time
Horses were not subject to body repair,
And with any little coming together
Nobody would just get off and stare,
To see if any damage for insurance
Which could land you up in court,
And possibly a more perilous ending
Than who was the driver at fault.

As maybe it would have been settled
By both parties going for their gun,
So one of them might be killed
Or be left lying out in the sun.
Thus not for them any third parties
With any witness statement need,
To ensure that justice was done
And the innocent would succeed.

But alas although we've moved on
From horseback to modern car.
Some still drive as if on the plains
When any street courtesy is far
Away from their immediate thought,
Which is to complete their drive
In the shortest time that's possible,
And just hope they stay alive.

Thus I would like to now see
Modern day sheriffs on our roads,
To monitor and punish rash cowboys
And enforce the highway codes.

--ooOoo--

I Hope it Doesn't Rain

At last everything is organised
With only a brief little pain,
And just one thing we can't control
So lets hope it doesn't rain.

For downpours have the ability
To literally put a damper on things,
However much all else is done
Any wet weather certainly brings,
Some slowing down or even stop
To all festivities that are planned.
So without a chance of recourse
Rain can take things out of hand.

For however we try to be stalwarts
And put on a brave, happy face,
Staying indoors to avoid the rain
Is really no great disgrace,
For the busy crowd hoped for
Will be that significantly less.
As slopping about in wet and mud
Just causes great distress.

So "I really hope it doesn't rain",
Is a regular offered up saying.
Because of all the consequences
So no wonder you are praying,
To have a pleasant weather day
Even if it's dry and very cold.
For we can deal with this
And see the intrepid and bold.

But rain can really ruin the day
Making everything all wet,
So I hope it doesn't rain at all
And a dry sunny day we get.

--ooOoo--

Pass Me the Remote

Little now is private or unmentioned
In the hard world of advertisement,
For it seems only pushing more sales
Can make these folks content.

So from painful periods in women
Where there is now so much advice,
To bladder weakness in us all
Which can be mopped up in a trice.
And that also goes for incontinence
Because there are many cures for this.
According that is to our advert guys
Who have products we can't miss.

Also they claim to having knowledge
Of products and help for nearly all,
But with some personal issues suffered
Their help and results are very small.
So our clever know-all's of the world
Have many suggestions to make money,
But little help on some vital needs
That to many just aren't funny.

So if you have a diarrhoea problem
They say there is something to halt,
Most embarrassing results of this
Alongside their laxatives that exult.
For as you become regular and smile
In your new freedom of motions.
Our advert guru's are now very sure
They can sell us all more potions.

Which then moves us on to our lives
Or perhaps I should say our dying,
Because they can organise the help
And that's without even trying.
Because it occurs to me these days
Everything personal comes to the fore.
So when these adverts come on now
I turn them off and shout "no more!"

But adverts say leave money in wills
So there will be no ensuing fight,
When you have left this world
Solicitors will show their might,
Ensuring with their cut of course
No family member will be left out.
Well that is the claim they make,
But I still retain some doubt.

Your funeral costs can cripple people
When you have the temerity to die,
So with a portion of your money
Funds can arrive in a blinking eye.
But as the adverts keep saying
They can arrange a full life cover,
Meaning you can be laid to rest
Without family killing one another.

But do we really need all these sales
On both our televisions and radio?
With leaking bladders and period pains
That apparently distress us so.
But do I really want to hear all this?
No I flipping well now don't,
So to shut them up and turn it off
Please pass me the remote.

--ooOoo--

Conspiracy

Just another doubting Thomas
Or maybe a pressure group belief,
That things didn't actually happen
Perhaps lied about through teeth,
That were firmly clenched closed
In an effort to keep in the lie,
About just what really did occur
With how, when and why?

For there are many conspiracy theories
On what actually had occurred
Because people refuse to believe in,
Any explanations or the word,
That says just what has happened
And in this or that manner.
But many people won't accept it
And hoist their doubting banner.

For lots of folks who won't accept
There was ever a moon landing,
Have various queries and disagree
With the story that is still standing,
Relating to a successful mission
To win first man on moon race,
For the conspiracy groups believe
It was a huge lie and disgrace.

Other doubts and questions cover
The twin towers attack event,
And the disappearance of Shergar
With all the money that was spent,
Trying to find him, and hasn't yet
Been resolved, whatever is now said.
And of course there are still those
Who don't think that Elvis is dead.

In history a strange story of a ship
That's shrouded in myth and mystery,
And loads of theories and guesses
On the Marie Celeste drifting at sea.

Another very long running debate
Which says no facts are crystal clear,
And that none of our great plays
Were really written by Shakespeare.
Also there's an unsolved mystery
That surrounds the Lord Lucan case.
Who suspiciously just vanished,
Some allege to save guilty face.

Though looking at huge controversies
And constant accusations of a lie,
Surrounds the mysterious tragic death
Of the very popular Lady Di.
Along with a callous assassination
Of President Kennedy in Dallas City,
Where theory arguments still rage
And very little signs of pity.

Flying saucers are regularly seen
But with no confirmations to explain,
Why circles in crop fields had appeared
So doubts and worries still remain.
Thus on and on debates will go
As conspiracy ideas continue to sprout,
For however mysteries are viewed
There will always be some doubt.

--ooOoo--

A Foot in the Grave?

I think we can probably all identify
At various times and situation,
With Richard Meldrew, that old misery
Starring in a t v soap procrastination,
In which life, and people for him
Are often far more than he can take.
With his famous phrase of frustration
Of "oh for goodness sake!"

Well I had one such similar period
On a recent Sunday afternoon,
When it seemed that I was surrounded
By every kind of cretin and loon.
For a sunny walk in a local park
Was spoilt by many things,
Including people reluctant to move
And blocking paths by the swings.

People and dogs that seemed to want
To have more leeway than you had,
Pulling their leads like a tripwire
Across your front, to make you mad,
Whilst idiotic owners look blithely on
As if it was some kind of joke,
Their little pooch would trip you up
Making you want to give them a poke.

Driving away could bring no peace
For it seemed this Sunday in the sun,
Had brought out many boy racers
Who thought crazy driving was fun,
Or even playing their little games
Completely daft and utterly dumb,
As they seemed intent to drive
Far too closely up your bum.

So deciding to have a relaxing pint
Into several pubs I did pull,
But many people had the same idea
As every pub car park was full.

Thus I decided to go back home
As no pleasure could I find or see,
But I did have a fleeting thought
That the only mad person was me.
But I'm really not sure the misery
In the t v soap would ever do this.
So on contemplating all the idiots,
Any blame of me I dismiss!

--ooOoo--

I Don't Belong Here

I just don't belong here now
For it really isn't me,
Amongst set forms and rules
With prudish hypocrisy.

Yes I hear you were mentioned
In that extreme high brow rag,
But I know you are phased by
My blatant flying of the flag,
With such widespread recognition
Of the common message I convey,
Made even worse when I rhyme
To totally conflict your way.

So best remain safe and secure
In your dusty, dreary case,
That is growing old and weary
Like dilemmas you now face,
Whilst trying to reach the baton
No longer being passed down.
That possibly may explain why
Your facade has a frown.

No I do not want to be here
In your outdated, crusty world,
Clinging to pompous regulations
Denying new ideas are unfurled,
Whilst demanding pieces of verse
Must adhere to a decreed way.
Thus I won't tarry or remain now
For your time has had its day!

--ooOoo--

Relay Race

A relay race is a team event
Consisting of races split into laps,
Run individually by team members
Who set off in staggered gaps,
So that all the participants,
Must run to waiting team mates
And pass a baton over to them,
Who then contest the race fate.

Obviously exchanging the baton
Is a crucial part of the race,
Because the speedier it is done
Will ensure the teams faster pace.
So the receiving person then sets off
On the next stage of the race trip.
But great care must be taken
Not to let the baton fall or slip.

For now we can clearly see
A relay race is not just about one
Specific team member over others,
For tactics may decide how it's run.
As some runners may be faster
But will still rely on the rest,
As important in the team effort,
When they try to be the best.

This then reminds me of our lives
When sometimes we need friends,
To stand by us and to help out
So all our heartache mends.
Thus just like the relay race
It's all a joint effort at times,
To get along lifetime roads
And find some happy climes.

So interactions are very important
With other people met on the way,
Just like the subtle baton change
Human greetings can make our day.
Thus be very conscious at all times
How important it is to share
Fellowship and courteous behaviour
And so win races when we care.

--ooOoo--

Wedding Dress

A wedding dress is a striking symbol
Invariably in a gleaming white,
To magnify the importance of the day
When you believe everything is right,
In your declaration of love and trust
You will live by all your years.
So allow credence and understanding
Of promises made before peers.

As sometimes attractions of the day
Can outweigh the reality of it all,
And lead to upset and heartaches
Should this wondrous day fall,
Into false hopes or expectations
That were never going to fulfil.
So shattered dreams and beliefs
Will taste a very bitter pill.

But back to that wedding gown,
The focus of desires and attention,
Worn as a beacon on the special day
So any doubts won't get a mention,
Or even really a fleeting thought
Compared to that wedding dress,
Now covering multitudes of thoughts
That you really should confess.

For maybe your day of stardom
Has more allure than what it means,
As people cheer and heap praise
On couples scarce past their teens.
Who face a future they think is sure
Although probably did not measure,
Their doubts and uncertainties
After a day of hopeful treasure.

So will that gleaming dress of white
Fit you well, and not just the size,
When real life or second thoughts
Make you begin to slowly realise,
How wearing the dress was easy
Though it covered so much concern,
And any fairytale life and endings
For so many crash and burn.

But you can keep that wedding dress
To always remember a special day,
Although possibly regrets and grief
Will often surface and betray,
The pretences that you put away
With those secrets you tried to hide,
As you acted out your greatest wish
To be that blushing bride.

--ooOoo--

Where?

Where have all my years gone
And can I please get them back?
I promise that I won't waste them
For I never let sad times stack,
Up too highly in my world
In those years of mine now past.
As I nearly always enjoyed myself
I guess why time went so fast.

So where have those years gone
Along with so many great days?
For I can still vividly remember
The songs and music that plays,
Like a magical memory jukebox
Rewinding much love and fun,
As they bring back situations
Where all was said and done.

Oh I can recall so many people
Sadly though some have gone,
Though their days are remembered
When they danced and faces shone,
From disco lights and silhouettes
Or maybe it was too much drink.

But that was in the distant past
Which makes me stop to think,
Just where have my years gone?
For it doesn't seem that long,
When my features were pristine
Like some newly written song.

Now as I look very fondly back
Over all those years I've had,
And people met and places seen
With more happier days than sad,
I feel my lifetime has stretched
Across many a stunning sunset,
But I hope for more to come
As I'm not ready to go just yet!

--ooOoo--

Filter

As I have to live within myself
I often contemplate my mood,
For although fairly rare with me
On some occasions I will brood.
And at those unusual times
When thoughts can be quite dark,
It's best that I restrain myself
As any comments could be stark.

Thus I need to have a tight filter
Controlling what I say or send,
In words or communication text
So no relationships I need to mend.
For like the saying about drunks
Who will tell the brutal truth,
On thoughts they once guarded
In an attempt to stay aloof.

Because that alcohol can loosen
The most protected of views,
Which can cause grave reactions
And some friends to lose.
Now I'm not saying I do that
But I do try hard to control,
Little opinions and any feelings
Not totally happy in my soul.

So when discontent or chagrin
Come calling to seek me out,
I have to be so very wary
My deep thoughts I don't spout.

--ooOoo--

Old Remedies

I was brought up on old remedies
With TCP and that Germolene,
Curing and helping those problems
Aches, bites and keeping cuts clean.
Now I'm not actually too sure
That they really saved many lives.
But one thing I'm certain of now,
Is that my health still thrives.

For with these two main treatments
You could gargle, wince or recover,
From lots of wounds and ailments
These great old remedies still cover.
Soothing, healing and calming down
Any nasty rash or spots attack,
To make you feel more comfortable
From head, toes and to the back.

But there were other remedies
That we were told would aid,
Any annoying minor little pains
Or silly accident wounds we made,
When careless or not watching
Just exactly what we were doing.
So when reaching for our saviours
Daft actions we were ruing.

Though of course those remedies
Couldn't cure all of our ills,
And sometimes we'd have to visit
The doctor for some pills.
Although Calamine did stop itches
With some butter easing burns,
So when all is said and done
Old remedies ease our concerns.

--ooOoo--

Northern Territories Nostalgia

We flew to Port Hedland from Perth
High up on Australia's western coast,
And picked up the hire car booked
That would give no cause to boast,
For it was a Toyota Yaris model
And an extremely gleaming white,
Which considering the local terrain
Didn't seem to me quite right.

Nothing wrong with the car at all,
Quite roomy for all of our gear,
But the colour was concerning
Although was told not to go near,
The famous Aussie outback roads
So very bumpy and an orange hue.
But when the tarmac roads run out,
What are you supposed to do?

I managed to stay on the good roads
Well most of the time that was,
But driving is not always easy
When travelling outside towns in Oz.
As what appears a normal route
Isn't always straight forward at all,
So I very soon learnt as well
Garages are hours between each call.

So back to the shiny white Yaris
I had given up on keeping clean,
But even though I had no chance
It was totally filthy when I had been
To a camp-site a bloke recommended
As just a bit off the main route.
Which turned out to be twelve miles
Along a vicious dirt track brute.

But because of the massive distances
That any camping areas were apart,
I had no chance to turn round in time
Or go back to make another start.
So down the bumpy road I went
With orange dust blowing all around,
To eventually be totally shocked
At just what it was I found.

Or more to the point didn't find
Because there wasn't much there,
Except loads of massive touring vans
And folks who met us with a stare
Between welcome and amazement
At our urban car and little tent.
Because this was semi permanent site
So for one night campers wasn't meant.

But we were made very welcome
Although only scant facilities for us,
Certainly not what we'd been informed
So we just got on without a fuss.
Cooking our great curry by the sea
And put up our tent just for sleeping,
But no room for anything much else
Which was in the car for safe keeping.

So after a nice evening and good sleep
It was goodbye and onto the bumpy road,
Resolving to listen to no more suggestions
About camping with our little load,
For we had decided it was prudent
To camp in more populated places,
Whenever it was we could do that
As there were miles of open spaces.

But a great time and adventure was had
And we got back all safe and sound,
Though we had to take care at times
And avoid crocodile infested ground.
Though back at the Port Hedland site
We got to see some official horse races,
So along with that and everything else
It is one of my favourite places.

--ooOoo--

Poet Reflects Your World

TRAGEDY

Letter From Afghanistan

A letter sent back from Afghanistan
Was not something to receive,
For it was probably tragic news
With no one coming home on leave.

Or a letter could be hand delivered
Titled on the "occasion of my death",
Penned for you by a loved one
And will take away your breath.
Because deploying troops are told
This was a letter they had to write,
Explaining their career commitments
And love for family while they fight.

Obviously when writing the letters
The authors hoped that it would be,
Just a precautionary exercise
And that nobody would need to see,
Their words of love and farewell
As they would return safe and sound.
So the "just in case it happened" mail,
Would not be homeward bound.

But sadly many such letters needed
Reluctant opening by shaking hands,
To a feeling we can only imagine
As nobody completely understands,
This sickening and traumatic time
When this letter home is read.
For it can only have dire meaning,
And that their loved one is dead.

Fortunately I never had to bear this
Although at times my heart would drop,
But I've met and seen such bereaved
And just know their pain won't stop.
So we must honour and appreciate
Our armed forces standing strong,
Who sacrifice and determine for us,
That very little will go wrong.

--ooOoo--

Absent

Every now and again I try
To complete a sort of roll call,
Of people that have slipped away
And I don't hear from at all.

Though this can be the normal
Sliding away by friends in life,
As we battle different challenges
That bring us joy or strife.
So if people should disappear
And now no longer are around,
You can only guess at reasons
For rumours may abound.

Though you occasionally get
Some news from recent meetings,
And so can learn from those
Of any messages or greetings.

For we live in a changing world
With people spreading out far more,
From areas they once grew up in
Before heading to another shore.

With multitudes of reasons why
Perhaps some they'd rather not say,
About why they've gone to ground
To surface on another day.

But with the internet and social media
Old friends and colleagues are found,
Though some sadly have passed away
And absent as the world goes round.

--ooOoo--

Bumpy Road

At times I get very weary now
Burdened by my heavy load,
Which often seems impossible
To carry further down the road.

But we all have our challenges
With various levels, large or small,
Because when our lots were decreed
It wasn't a simple one size fits all.
Thus the smallest may carry most
And the largest just a lightweight.
But this harsh world still ordains
That we must stand up straight.

Although of course we struggle on
With the many demands of us,
So we do our best to meet them
With just the minimum of fuss.
For sympathy comes slow at times
When people only see our outside,
So brave folk will try to smile
Driven by their stubborn pride.

Thus down our weary way we go
Some moving fast, and others slow,
With those who have to pack it in
Convinced that they can never win.
But life requires that we must try
And with no explanations of why,
We are still compelled to live
Even if having little left to give.
So gird your loins to fight the fight,
And try hard with all your might.

--ooOoo--

Expiry Date

Well I nearly didn't recognise you
As I hardly know your face,
With some strange look across it
That I can't seem to place.
Now looking at that expression
I don't know what it can show,
As some dark, angry countenance
Replaces a face that used to glow.

And this shallow guilty reflection
Quickly runs away behind your eyes,
Which allows this sad subsidence
To complete a bleak disguise.
For there's clearly been some expiry
Like a product going out of date.
And I can only sadly imagine
What brought about this fate.

For I used to love you deeply
As you showed that you loved me,
But this has obviously well passed
So the whole world can now see,
That I don't know you any more
Having lost you some time ago,
Going away to seek your sunshine
But only finding life's woe.

Thus I cannot connect with you
In any nearby or distant way,
For your haggard look of shame
Has seen you suffered many a day.
So how can love that shone so bright
Get replaced by your face so dire,
But we could never have guessed
Our great love would expire.

So now I just don't know you
And I've never seen that face,
Which tries to hide embarrassment
But only marks out your disgrace.
Thus many a moon has gone down
Over all those ecstatic years,
Now leaving you as an expiry date
With only days full of tears.

--ooOoo--

What a Piece of .....

The wonderfully expansive Shakespeare
Wrote magnificent words on everything,
From loves joy, sadness to tragedy
Using words that made hearts sing.

One such speech and quote from Hamlet
Is "what a piece of work is man",
Going on to exult, but question
As to why man kills all he can.
With the murder of animals for gain
And shredding world treasure to the bone.
But worse than this is man's wars
With people keen to cast the first stone.

Bombings, shooting and killings abound
In almost accepted daily news,
When man's bigotry, racism and hatred
Surfaces across our planet, and spews
Mass slaughter, pain and carnage,
Even now on Easter's religious day
Sri Lanka is decimated by bombs,
As evil scum murder their way.

Oh what a piece of work is man?
Although I could answer profane,
But outrage and contemptuous disgust
Now seems is uttered in vain.
For our world drops in downward spiral
Lemming like, in a desire to die.
While in some places across the globe
A few people cry in anguish, "why"?

So maybe I can pose an answer
In that mutual respect has now gone.
A respect for man, animals and our world,
When for so many centuries joy shone.
But maybe it is not yet all lost
As some are intent to put things right,
So I will stand alongside them until
We stop man being a piece of shite!

--ooOoo--

Clown at a Wake

Some events in life should be serious
With all due decorum they require,
As we try to meet appropriate needs
Of settled behaviour and smart attire.

But human nature is not all like this
And there will always be the clown,
Who despite the pleas of others
Can bring any situation down,
By maybe having too much drink
Or an over-loud spoken word,
To cause a dispute or argument
When his crass comment is heard.

This can then very soon escalate
Into a massive incident and row,
Whilst the culprit looks bewildered
At the scene, and wonders how,
Such an unseemly occurrence
Could have actually happened here.
But being oblivious of any blame
Will calmly sip another beer.

So there's always the one in a crowd
Who can make discontent bloom,
Having notorious ability to start
A fight in an empty room.
Whether it is the demon drink
Or their actions that sadly sway,
The appropriate peace and quiet
And spoil a respectful day.

Thus be careful of your guest list
And just who is going to be there,
For our loose cannon clown
Can create havoc without care.

--ooOoo--

With No Warning

We never know when our time is up
Or that exact moment we will die,
And to make it all more complex
We may have no reason as to why.
Because our expectation is to live
A long life as in healthcare we're skilled,
So may beat most illness for a while,
But can also be accidentally killed.

For tragedies will always happen to us
Whether at work, war or in a car,
So that our passing may be sudden
And people may not know where we are.

Perhaps because it was undecided
Or maybe a secret for deceit,
When having a covert relationship
And a lover you went to meet.
So nobody will know the location
Or why there and for what reason.
Just a confirmation of your expiry
But no mention yet of treason.

For that will come much later
When questions are all looked at,
As to why, how and for what
Had you been in that place and sat,
Somewhere that was not known at all
To your close family and friends.
Who are only beginning to realise now,
You went there for your own ends.

Thus this leads to more questions
Like would you still be alive today,
If not going to the unknown place
And why did you not say
That you would be going somewhere
Not previously having a mention?
So was the reason for this silence
Exactly your deceitful intention?

Therefore many secrets can leak
If a rapid death strikes at will,
And if this exposes a betrayal
It can taste a very bitter pill.
But of course all sudden deaths
May not have any such asides,
So just an unexpected passing
As from this world we slide.

--ooOoo--

Blemishes or Insanity?

Nothing in life is ever perfect
For every flower bed has a weed,
And the most ornate of ponds
Will suffer their share of reed.
So accept the ways of this world
And its complexity of how made.
For even if you're benign and kind,
Someone will rain on your parade.

Although perhaps it's not the fault
Of the world and how created,
As bad times will often infiltrate it
With any remedies only belated,
In resolving the upset or trauma
Our life may let out of the can.
But most blame for imperfections
Should be laid at the feet of man.

For his jealousy, greed and vanity
Of being greatest and having more,
Than anyone else's riches and land
Will so often lead to war.

Though maybe it is quite simple
And just an obsession to be the best,
Which The Bard describes succinctly
As never being at their hearts rest,
If beholding greater than themselves
Although every person has their skill,
Which our unsatisfied man can't see
So it continues to make him ill.

Meanwhile the riches and splendour
Of the wonderful world must pay,
For the destruction and atrocities
When man wants to have his way.
So best to admire your flower bed
And pond complete with its reed.
Because these slight blemishes
Won't cause our world to bleed.

--ooOoo--

Quiet Joker

The life and soul of any party
And can be everyone's best friend,
But nobody knows, or sees the time
That his darkness will descend.
Because he has hidden demons
That the outside world won't know,
For he keeps this secret safe
And will never let it show.

Now there's been a run of comedians
Funny people who couldn't cope,
But had filled audiences with laughter
Though inside they'd given up hope.
For it seemed their fame had increased
Their inner misery and darkest thought.
Until they sadly had to announce it,
Or on a suicide spire were caught.

So on the outside it seems easier
For our jovial and jolly man,
Who has no world wide standing
Or is subject of inquisitive scan.
But it doesn't seem any simpler
Dealing with his life contradiction,
Where even if people were aware
They would treat it as pure fiction.

So away from parties and friends
He struggles on in his quicksand,
Trapped between being a joker
And a world that can't understand,
How our joker and mega character
Who makes people laugh over again,
Is crushed in a world of dark torture
And an excruciating inner pain.

--ooOoo--

Bird Songs

I think nearly everybody loves birds
Maybe even more so when they sing,
To enrich us with wonderful sounds
And the simple pleasure this brings.
For if hopping about in ones or twos
Or gathering in a great flock,
To me there is a sense of delight
As my heartstrings they unlock.

Not everyone's personal approval
Is a famed dawn chorus birds present,
For some say that it wakes them up
But I think this sound is heaven sent.
As these innocuous creatures bob about
In the decreed circle of their being,
Minding their own business and needs
That enhances ears and our seeing.

Because it seems very much to me
That every action has a meaning,
So no greed or jealousy occurs
If their simple needs are gleaning.
Of course there's an odd little squabble
As of most creatures wanting to mate,
But these are confined to necessity
And little involvement of others fate.

So their songs and cries have purpose
Whilst giving delight to our ears,
Being even heard in battlefield lulls
Of many conflicts down the years.
Though there is an eerie silence
In certain places of a cruel world,
Like Auschwitz and Belsen horrors
When man's inhumanity was unfurled.

For even the birds won't sing there
Whilst still living local and move,
About in lessons to our cruelty
For hurtful crimes they try to sooth,
Taught by the smallest of creatures
As our message of love and peace,
Who through their beautiful songs
Implore mankind's wars to cease.

So don't ever begrudge any birds
A life, intrusion or their songs,
Because compared with man's evil
They've committed very few wrongs.

--ooOoo--

You Made Your Bed

You made your bed so lie in it,
As the old-time saying goes.
In a quite damning exclamation
Aimed, and thus delivered at those,
Who maybe took a chance
About a decision or a choice.
Sometimes leading to heartache
Or perhaps occasions to rejoice.

So possibly the receiver of,
The "well you made your bed",
Perhaps felt very pressurised
And only took a chance instead,
Of sticking to a safer place
That then really appealed.
But a chance had to be taken on,
Though not what it revealed.

Now some people make decisions
Against all sensible argument,
When going out on chancy limbs
In a steadfast manner of intent,
Possibly to shock or make a show
Against accepted points of view,
So they are prepared take blame
For opposite things they do.

But while we salute their bravery
Trying to cock snoops at convention.
If going wrong for them at the end
There's no sympathy for intention.

And although that's mostly the case,
Some people have to take a chance.
Because it's the lesser of two evils
Which makes them take a stance,
That may seem on the surface
A choice of how making their bed.
But in some extreme situations
If they don't they might be dead.

Because our world isn't totally safe
And terrorism and criminals thrive,
So at times simple innocent folks
Have to take risks to stay alive.
And if looks like they deserve trouble
For making of their metaphoric bed,
Give them the benefit of doubt
And having to listen to their head.

--ooOoo--

Surfers Against Sewage

An excellent charity called S A S
Is dedicated to cleaning up our mess
Collecting in seas and on the beaches,
With warnings, and education that teaches
That we can no longer just not care,
And dump waste and rubbish everywhere,
To pollute our glorious world treasures
Which have worth beyond measures.

So this group of dedicated guys
Will spread the word and always tries,
To get people to learn and understand
Not to bury their heads in the sand,
And realise just what is going wrong
In real life, and not merely a song,
About how seas and creatures die
So we can no longer stand idly by.

Because the dangers are getting worse
Than when first recognised as a curse,
By a small committed group in a hall
Who viewed with dismay and appal,
The worlds messy and polluted sea
Where they hoped to surf happily.
But disgusted by filth they got right out
To make a protest group come about.

Thus now the message is sent out clear
About our world we should hold dear,
For generations to love and appreciate
And not leave tarnished in a dirty state,
Of plastic, rubbish and sewage raw
We don't want to tolerate anymore.
So we will battle with all our might,
Please come and join us in the fight.

The Pool and the Leaves

There's a camp site by my French place
With a small, round swimming pool,
That gets leaves dropping in it
Which is not too good at all.
So every morning of each day
The site manager would get them out.
Which was appreciated by swimmers,
And of that there is no doubt.

He also used to maintain the camp
Making sure everything was clean,
Not just because it was his job
But so it looked nice when seen.
Though sadly he is no longer here
For cruel cancer took him away,
And those leaves are still dropping
But the pool gets cleared each day.

So as I pass, or sit with a drink
At the site bar that's just nearby,
I often get to wonder about life
Which can often make us cry.
For the man who cleaned the pool
Was nowhere near my years,
Yet was removed from life early
Condemning his family to tears.

Now many of us will leave things
That occupy ourselves and time,
And when we have left the world
We hope memories remain sublime.
So for me it's my words and poems
About love, life and she who grieves,
Over things still here without us
Like the man who cleared the leaves.

--ooOoo--

Slipping Away

I can't reach you much anymore
You are just too far away,
And I know you're not understanding
Hardly anything I now say.

Though if I can keep it simple
It's still possible to get through,
But nothing like a conversation
Regarding things we used to do,
With all the places that we saw
And amazing experiences we had,
That now you can't remember
And that is so very sad.

An independence held so firm
Is now replaced by gross anxiety,
For you question every little task
That is now very hard to see.
Although there are fleeting bits
Of the person you once were,
For resistive and stubbornness stay
But so much is just a blur.

Thus we contemplate our years
And what will happen to us,
But should it be more adversity
We must confront it without fuss.
Though that is quite easy to say
For me who is so far unaffected,
By ageing pains and conditions
That have not with me connected.

But be sure any oncoming illnesses
Affecting my mind and health abilities,
Will be robustly resisted and fought
Before I go down on my knees.

--ooOoo--

Mobilecide

Suicide Is intentionally killing yourself
When towards that sad act you slide.
But now we have another way to die,
Unintentional, and called "mobilecide"

For mobilecide comes from the misuse,
Of your companion, the mobile phone.
With all the latest gadgets and devices
That checks you're in touch and not alone.
The problem with this is very simple,
In that you must look at your screens
At almost continual times and occasions,
To ensure you know what it means!

There are several forms of mobilecide
And can depend on where you are,
But by far the most certain, lethal way
Is to use your phone and drive a car.

A quick look at it, or maybe make a call
Or perhaps temptation to send a text,
So that your eyes are off your driving
And have no clues to what happens next.
You are not attending to the road
So you swerve to left, or maybe right,
At an oncoming car, maybe a big van
But each could spell the last goodnight!

Of course other people may be involved,
Not fault of theirs they're in the way.
But your averted eyes don't see them
And after you hit them, what do you say?
"Oh God I really didn't mean it"
No intention for this at all.
You got distracted by your phone,
So you killed them and hit the wall.

By walking you are not in the clear
If constantly at your phone you look,
Because the unseen driver who hits you
Was surprised by the chance you took,
A pedestrian without any awareness
Of a highway code you may have read.
For to go blindly cross the road
Ensures you will soon end up dead!

Thus questions must be asked of the mobile,
Is it for fun, information, or tears.
For giving it attention, and not yourself
Means you won't live many years.

--ooOoo--

Beyond the Facade

A profile of beaming countenance
Is portrayed for us one and all.
But it's hard to maintain consistency
That will always be there to fool,
Us humble and yet knowing public
You try so very hard to convince.
But I saw your fleeting scowl
And have been suspicious since.

For the best Shakespearian actors
Would find it hard to maintain,
This adopted role continually
With never a slip up or stain,
That can blemish or give a clue
Ubout your facade so benign,
Which you have decided to wear
To presents a look so fine.

Though I did see that little slip
Before a quickly snatched up smile,
Immediately replaced the facial error
Thus was only there for a brief while
Before being replaced and corrected,
So you thought was safely restored.
But I have lightning observations
And saw that you were bored.

So now there is an understanding
That all is not as it is presented,
For probably many various reasons
But my guess is you just resented,
A life and occupation that maybe
Would not be your chosen line.
Thus I think you now cover this
With more than one extra wine.

--ooOoo--

Don't Turn the Lights Out

When life gets difficult and frustrating
People's attitudes will become hard,
And more protective of their situations
So being fearful they prepare to guard,
Their family home and possessions
Which of course is totally right.
But this must be done with caution
And not turn out every light.

Because if a country or an area
Feels threatened and likely to lose,
Any jobs, peace or way of life
It may be encouraged to choose,
One side and take on arguments
Which were not the case before,
Extreme and determined radicals
Wanted to engage in forms of war.

Thus everyone begins to get paranoid
And fear their rights may be curtailed,
Fuelled by provoking propaganda
Saying a peaceful stance has failed.
But in the background of this unrest
Are some folks with hearts still stout,
Who are worried and try to warn
Against madness turning lights out.

For we have been taught by history
About whipped-up hate and racist acts,
That can turn people against each other
Without really knowing all the facts.
But can lead to unspeakably cruel deeds
Which are frightening without a doubt.
Because we have seen the worst of man
If turning lights of fellowship out.

So we must try hard to remember
The dark times we can get into,
When hatred, lies and extremism
Became traits men went on to pursue,
Leading to racist actions and events
Which caused sad gruesome sights.
Thus we should recollect before
We turn out all the world's lights.

--ooOoo--

Fortitude

The shrieking wind shook off the hand
Desperately clinging to the rail,
And threatened to flatten him
For fighting was to no avail,
As weakened frame and battered mind
Could offer no more defence,
Against the elements bombardment
So now resistance made no sense.

But a defiant spark was remaining
While a strong will said hold on,
And struggle to the bitter end
When all hope has finally gone.
Because man has a deep inner will
That can achieve huge success,
When all has appeared hopeless
And seemed an impossible mess.

So what is it that drives us on
Like the intrepid case as above?
Well I believe it is our fine spirit
And a considered belief that love
Can help us overcome diversity
And everything that life can throw.
But obviously there are times
When we just have to let go.

Though meanwhile we can take a lead
From courageous exploring heroes,
Who forged new paths and discoveries
So that everywhere man now goes,
He has the lessons on fortitude
Taught by Trojans from the past,
Who used love and determination
To teach how to make it last.

--ooOoo--

Brexit Wounds

I suppose I must comment on Brexit
As nearly everyone else has now,
But I don't like to get political
Or take sides in this great row.

For it was all meant to be so easy
A simple choice of in or out.
Well if you believed what was said
And people all knew everything about,
This sort of modern day exodus
With music and banners flying high.
But we find three long years later
The Brexit Ark is high and dry.

Thus we do a sort of Hokey Cockey
In out and shake it all about then.
But it seems more like pass the parcel,
And you're out if the music stops when
You are the one left holding the baby,
Or more like booby in this sad case.
Because instead of showing pride
We're now a world wide disgrace.

Close friends have now fallen out
In this populations sad civil war.
With the tragic and biggest irony
Is people have forgotten just what for,
We were involved in this journey
Full of national and patriotic hope,
That somehow has now slipped away
Like an elusive bar of soap.

And whilst mentioning slipping away
It's not just the soap we cannot find,
For all the major Brexit protagonists
Have run away, or lost their mind.
So in this much argued situation
With even families now all at odds,
Nothing remains constant in this farce
Between both victims and the gods.

So let's hope we can still be delivered
With our exit wounds nicely healed,
And that all the casualties and bankrupt
Number those to who leaving so appealed.
For when we slide and limp to any finish
Instead of parading a Grand March refrain,
That was fully expected and prayed for
It's maybe best if we start again?

--ooOoo--

A Throw of the Dice

Lured and beguiled by temptations net
We may hear sirens alluring sounds,
For responses wake excited feelings
As our heartbeat skips and pounds.

Thus again loves trap is baited
For times that can be very nice,
So take that moment of reflection
Before any rolling of the dice.
For the lure of promised pleasure
With a gorgeous sight of wonder,
Blinds any awareness sighted
So with our dice we blunder.

Oh, but there is brief satisfaction
And ecstasy to make you smile,
Though make the very most of it
As it will only last a while,
Before reality and acceptance call
To tell you of impending fate,
As you took a chance on rolling dice
So now it is too late.

For a moment you may look back
And consider what has been done,
Because the light is dawning now
That you have nowhere left to run,
As the dye is now finally cast
Just as you did with those dice,
And now regretting your deaf ears,
On all that good advice.

So just where have you landed,
And what will happen now?
Well, you still have a brief chance
Thus it's best to make your bow,
For you gave into temptation
Ignoring what friends had to say.
Now sadly you will remember,
About the dog who had his day!

--ooOoo--

****

Poet Reflects Your World

APPENDIX

Continued compliments and feedback to me on my poetry recounts that many people like to work out the meanings of my poems for themselves, or even attach their own personal experiences and thoughts as they resonate with them.

I think that is truly wonderful, but for other folks who like to seek my reasons and explanations for them, please review my comments below.

As I tend to write spontaneously and often on subjects that have really emoted me, I will mostly "nail my thoughts in", so most of the themes are quite clear or self explanatory.

However the poems listed in this appendix below are the less obvious topics and thoughts, but please add any personalisation or special meaning that they have for you individually too, as I will feel honoured!

Mary Go Round:-   The complexities of attraction

Loves Illusion Confusion:-   That we can often be be blinkered and make wrong decisions with love, but it is better than having never tried

Hypnotic Dance:-   Reflecting on a fantasy

Hand Fight at O K Sauce Table:- My parody of the Gunfight at O K Coral (but this has actually happened)

The Lonely Life of a Lemon:- As most people will have "felt like a lemon" at some time, why do we ostracise them? This is my plea for lemons then.

The Man Who Has Seen Everything:- About the shallow people living in their small, safe world preferring to think they know everything, but are frightened to take on the unknowns elsewhere.

Damsons and Distress:- Sadly a true story of mine from the late seventies

Cowboys and Motorists:- On a particularly bad day for other motorists driving behaviours, this conceptual comparison arrived!

Pass Me the Remote:- A largely straightforward thought from one day of "too much information" bombardment about "body function failures, funeral costs and life insurance" advertisements.

A Foot in the Grave:- On confronting how life can sometimes compel us all to be like the miserable Richard Meldrew of "One Foot in the Grave" television programme.

I Don't Belong Here:- My response to crusty, prudish views about (mine?) down to earth poetry, and also perhaps my somewhat startling progress in a very short time.

Wedding Dress:- A take on the allure, hypocrisy and "chasing down the aisle" that proceeds many weddings?

Bumpy Road:- On the demands of life, often with no quarter given, and maybe much worse for those that the road is hardest.

Expiry Date:- A reflection on a long ago betrayal that rebounded, and poem was inspired by a Joe Cocker song.

What a Piece of....:- My revulsion of many destructive situations in our world today, and just how many aspects and ways man seeks to remove our priceless world treasures and creatures!

With No Warning:- That life can be very fragile and we can depart it at any time, so best we ensure our "papers" are in order?

Blemishes or Insanity?:- Indulge the blemishes and imperfections of life that are so much better than the obscene demands and destruction wrought by greedy and selfish men.

You Made Your Bed:- My note that sometimes we have to make our "bed of life" under circumstances that are not our choice.

The Pool and the Leaves:- A sad reminder to me that what we do, and how we deal with our life, remains more than us.

Slipping Away:- On the destruction of people that dementia can cause.

Don't Put the Lights Out:- A warning that it is too easy to make conflict over very little, and the disastrous consequences it can lead to.

More?

I hope that you enjoyed this book
For I tried to pack lots in,
With various themes in sections
So you can choose where to begin,
And take yourself on journeys
Or if you wished to, just remain.
For I have other books out now,
Thus you can have it all again.

With poems to make you romantic
And some verses if you feel deep.
Others will make you look back on life,
Even smile when you go to sleep.

Of course Ted and Beth will feature
I can hardly leave them out.
As surely they'll have new adventures,
Well of this I have no doubt!
And I will have new observations
I glean from scanning life's tree.
Take care then you are not included
When I write down what I see.

So please look at my other books
And support "Help for Heroes" too,
For all my sales donate to them
From my poems I write for you.

You can get books from my website online
And to message me direct will be fine.
With every contact listed below
Including all that you need to know,
To search for me on the Amazon club
Or just come and find me down the pub!

My other books are:-
Poetic Views of Life
MORe Poetic Views of Life
Reviews of Life in Verse
Life Scene in Verse
Life Presented in Verse
Poet Reveals All

My Contacts:-
Email = lw1800@hotmail.co.uk
Amazon authors page= Laurie Wilkinson
Facebook page = The Psychy Poet Laurie
Wilkinson
Facebook page =Ted n Beth of Laurie the Poet
Website = www.psychypoet.com

Laurie Wilkinson

Poet Reflects Your World

Laurie Wilkinson

Lightning Source UK Ltd.
Milton Keynes UK
UKHW040707121119
353313UK00011B/59/P